Contents

W9-AVE-903

Acknowledgments

The publisher would like to thank Nestlé USA
for the use of their recipe in this publication.

Marshmallow Fudge Sundae Cupcakes

1 package (18¼ ounces) chocolate cake mix, plus ingredients to prepare mix

2 packages (4 ounces each) waffle bowls

40 large marshmallows

1 jar (8 ounces) hot fudge topping

1¼ cups whipped topping

¼ cup sprinkles

1 jar (10 ounces) maraschino cherries

1. Preheat oven to 350°F. Lightly spray 20 standard (2½-inch) muffin pan cups with nonstick cooking spray.

2. Prepare cake mix according to package directions. Spoon batter into prepared muffin cups, filling ⅔ full. Bake about 20 minutes or until toothpick inserted into centers comes out clean. Cool in pans on wire rack about 10 minutes.

3. Remove cupcakes from pans; place one cupcake in each waffle bowl. Place waffle bowls on baking sheet. Top each cupcake with 2 marshmallows and return to oven for 2 minutes or until marshmallows are slightly softened.

4. Remove lid from fudge topping; heat in microwave on HIGH 10 seconds or until softened. Top each cupcake with 2 teaspoons fudge topping, 1 tablespoon whipped topping, sprinkles and cherry.

Makes 20 cupcakes

Chocolate

Give Me S'More Muffins

2 cups graham cracker crumbs
⅓ **cup sugar**
2 teaspoons baking powder
⅓ **cup mini chocolate chips**
1 egg
¾ **cup milk**
24 milk chocolate candy kisses, unwrapped
2 cups minature marshmallows

1. Preheat oven to 350°F. Line 24 mini (1¾-inch) muffin pan cups with foil baking cups.

2. Combine graham cracker crumbs, sugar, baking powder and chips in medium bowl. Whisk egg into milk and stir into crumb mixture until blended.

3. Spoon batter into prepared muffin cups, filling about ½ full. Press chocolate kiss into each cup. Press 4 marshmallows around each chocolate kiss. Bake 10 to 12 minutes or until marshmallows are lightly browned. Cool 10 minutes in pan. Remove muffins to wire rack; cool completely.

Makes 24 mini muffins

Chocolate

5

Choco–Zucchini Muffins

2⅓ cups all-purpose flour

1¼ cups sugar

⅓ cup unsweetened cocoa powder

2 teaspoons baking powder

1½ teaspoons ground cinnamon

1 teaspoon baking soda

½ teaspoon salt

1 cup sour cream

½ cup vegetable oil

2 eggs, beaten

¼ cup milk

1 cup *each* milk chocolate chips and shredded zucchini

1. Preheat oven to 400°F. Line 18 standard (2½-inch) muffin pan cups with paper baking cups.

2. Combine flour, sugar, cocoa, baking powder, cinnamon, baking soda and salt in large bowl. Combine sour cream, oil, eggs and milk in small bowl until blended; stir into flour mixture just until moistened. Fold in chocolate chips and zucchini. Spoon into prepared muffin cups, filling ½ full.

3. Bake 18 to 20 minutes or until toothpick inserted into centers comes out clean. Cool in pan on wire rack 5 minutes. Remove muffins from pan to rack; cool completely. Store tightly covered at room temperature.

Makes 18 muffins

Chocolate

White Chocolate Chunk Muffins

2½ cups all-purpose flour

1 cup packed light brown sugar

⅓ cup unsweetened cocoa powder

2 teaspoons baking soda

½ teaspoon salt

1⅓ cups buttermilk

¼ cup (½ stick) plus 2 tablespoons butter, melted

2 eggs, beaten

1½ teaspoons vanilla

1½ cups chopped white chocolate

1. Preheat oven to 400°F. Grease 12 jumbo (3½-inch) muffin pan cups.

2. Combine flour, sugar, cocoa, baking soda and salt in large bowl. Combine buttermilk, butter, eggs and vanilla in small bowl until blended. Stir into flour mixture just until moistened. Fold in white chocolate. Spoon into prepared muffin cups, filling ½ full.

3. Bake 25 to 30 minutes or until toothpick inserted into centers comes out clean. Cool in pan on wire rack 5 minutes. Remove muffins from pan to rack; cool 10 minutes.

Makes 12 muffins

chocolate

Double Malted Cupcakes

2 cups all-purpose flour

¼ cup plus 1 tablespoon malted milk powder, divided

2 teaspoons baking powder

¼ teaspoon salt

1¾ cups granulated sugar

¾ cup (1½ sticks) butter, softened and divided

1 cup milk

2½ teaspoons vanilla, divided

3 egg whites

4 ounces milk chocolate candy bar, broken into chunks

¼ cup whipping cream

1¾ cups powdered sugar

30 malted milk balls

1. Preheat oven to 350°F. Line 30 standard (2½-inch) muffin pan cups with paper baking cups.

2. Combine flour, ¼ cup malted milk powder, baking powder and salt in large bowl; set aside. Beat sugar and ½ cup butter in medium bowl with electric mixer at medium speed 1 minute. Add milk and 1½ teaspoons vanilla; beat at low speed 30 seconds. Gradually beat in flour mixture until blended. Add egg whites; beat 1 minute. Spoon batter into prepared muffin cups, filling ⅔ full.

3. Bake 20 minutes or until golden brown. Cool in pans on wire racks 10 minutes. Remove cupcakes to racks; cool completely.

4. Meanwhile, melt chocolate and remaining ¼ cup butter in heavy medium saucepan over low heat, stirring frequently. Stir in cream, remaining 1 tablespoon malted milk powder and remaining 1 teaspoon vanilla; mix well. Gradually stir in powdered sugar. Cook 4 to 5 minutes, stirring constantly, until smooth; remove from heat. Refrigerate 20 minutes.

5. Frost cupcakes; decorate with malted milk balls.

Makes 30 cupcakes

Chocolate

Mini Turtle Cupcakes

1 package (21½ ounces) brownie mix plus ingredients to prepare mix

½ cup chopped pecans

1 cup prepared dark chocolate frosting

½ cup coarsely chopped pecans, toasted*

12 caramels

1 to 2 tablespoons whipping cream

*Spread pecans in shallow baking pan. Bake in preheated 350°F oven 5 to 10 minutes or until fragrant, stirring occasionally.

1. Preheat oven to 350°F. Line 54 mini (1½-inch) muffin pan cups with paper baking cups.

2. Prepare brownie mix according to package directions. Stir in ½ cup chopped pecans. Spoon batter into prepared muffin cups, filling ⅔ full.

3. Bake 18 minutes or until toothpick inserted into centers comes out clean. Cool in pans on wire racks 5 minutes. Remove cupcakes to racks; cool completely.

4. Spread frosting over cupcakes; top with ½ cup toasted pecans. Combine caramels and 1 tablespoon cream in small saucepan. Cook and stir over low heat until caramels melt and mixture is smooth. Add additional 1 tablespoon cream if necessary. Spoon caramel over cupcakes. Store at room temperature up to 24 hours. *Makes 54 mini cupcakes*

Chocolate

Chocolate Frosted
Peanut Butter Cupcakes

⅓ cup butter, softened
⅓ cup plus 3 tablespoons creamy peanut butter, divided
½ cup granulated sugar
¼ cup packed brown sugar
2 eggs
1 teaspoon vanilla
1¾ cups all-purpose flour
1½ teaspoons baking powder
¼ teaspoon salt
1¼ cups plus 4 tablespoons milk, divided
4 cups powdered sugar
⅓ cup cocoa powder

1. Preheat oven to 350°F. Line 18 standard (2½-inch) muffin pan cups with foil baking cups.

2. Beat butter and ⅓ cup peanut butter in large bowl with electric mixer at medium speed until smooth. Beat in sugars until well mixed. Beat in eggs and vanilla. Combine flour, baking powder and salt in medium bowl. Add flour mixture to peanut butter mixture alternately with 1¼ cups milk, beginning and ending with flour mixture. Spoon batter into prepared muffin cups, filling ⅔ full.

3. Bake 23 to 25 minutes or until toothpicks inserted into centers come out clean. Cool in pans on wire racks 10 minutes. Remove cupcakes to racks; cool completely.

4. Combine powdered sugar, cocoa powder, remaining 4 tablespoons milk and remaining 3 tablespoons peanut butter in large bowl. Beat with electric mixer at low speed until smooth. Beat in additional milk, 1 tablespoon at a time, until frosting is desired consistency. Frost cupcakes.

Makes 18 cupcakes

Chocolate

Chocolate Malts

1¾ cups cake flour
¾ teaspoon baking soda
½ teaspoon salt
1¼ cups granulated sugar, divided
2 eggs, at room temperature
⅓ cup vegetable oil
1 cup low-fat buttermilk
¼ cup chocolate malted milk powder plus additional for garnish
1 teaspoon vanilla
1 cup thawed frozen whipped topping
½ cup marshmallow creme
Chopped malted milk balls

1. Preheat oven to 350°F. Grease and flour 12 standard (2½-inch) muffin pan cups.

2. Sift flour, baking soda and salt together in bowl. Stir in ¾ cup sugar; set aside. Beat eggs and remaining ½ cup sugar in large bowl with electric mixer at medium-high speed 3 minutes until light and glossy. Reduce mixer speed to low. Add ⅓ of flour mixture; beat until thick. Add oil; beat until smooth. Combine buttermilk, milk powder and vanilla in small bowl; stir until milk powder is dissolved. Add ⅓ of buttermilk mixture to batter; beat until smooth. Add remaining flour mixture alternating with remaining buttermilk mixture, beating well after each addition. Divide batter evenly among prepared muffin cups.

3. Bake about 25 minutes or until toothpick inserted into centers comes out clean. Cool in pan on wire rack 15 minutes. Remove cupcakes to rack; cool completely.

4. Combine whipped topping and marshmallow creme in medium bowl; stir until well blended. Frost cupcakes; sprinkle with malted milk balls.

Makes 12 cupcakes

chocolate

Holiday Pumpkin Muffins

2½ cups all-purpose flour
1 cup packed light brown sugar
1 tablespoon baking powder
1 teaspoon ground cinnamon
½ teaspoon *each* ground nutmeg and ground ginger
¼ teaspoon salt
1 cup solid-pack pumpkin (not pumpkin pie filling)
¾ cup milk
2 eggs
6 tablespoons butter, melted
⅔ cup roasted, salted pumpkin seeds, divided
½ cup golden raisins

1. Preheat oven to 400°F. Grease 18 standard (2¾-inch) muffin pan cups.

2. Combine flour, brown sugar, baking powder, cinnamon, nutmeg, ginger and salt in large bowl. Stir pumpkin, milk, eggs and melted butter in medium bowl until well blended. Stir pumpkin mixture into flour mixture. Mix just until ingredients are moistened. Stir in ⅓ cup pumpkin seeds and raisins. Spoon into prepared muffin cups, filling ⅔ full. Sprinkle remaining pumpkin seeds over muffin batter.

3. Bake 15 to 18 minutes or until toothpick inserted into centers comes out clean. Cool in pans on wire racks 10 minutes. Remove muffins from pans to racks; cool completely. Store in airtight container.   *Makes 18 muffins*

Holiday

Cranberry Pecan Muffins

1¾ cups all-purpose flour

½ cup packed light brown sugar

2½ teaspoons baking powder

½ teaspoon salt

¾ cup milk

¼ cup (½ stick) butter, melted

1 egg, beaten

1 cup chopped fresh cranberries

⅓ cup chopped pecans

1 teaspoon grated lemon peel

1. Preheat oven to 400°F. Grease 36 mini (1¾-inch) muffin cups.

2. Combine flour, brown sugar, baking powder and salt in large bowl. Combine milk, butter and egg in small bowl until blended; stir into flour mixture just until moistened. Fold in cranberries, pecans and lemon peel. Spoon into prepared muffin cups, filling almost full.

3. Bake 15 to 17 minutes or until toothpick inserted into centers comes out clean. Remove from pans; cool on wire racks. *Makes 36 muffins*

Holiday

73

Snowman Cupcakes

1 package (18¼ ounces) yellow or white cake mix, plus
   ingredients to prepare mix

2 containers (16 ounces each) vanilla frosting

4 cups flaked coconut

15 large marshmallows

15 miniature chocolate covered peanut butter cups

   Red cinnamon candies and pretzel sticks

   Green and red decorating gels

1. Preheat oven to 350°F. Line 15 standard (2½-inch) muffin pan cups and 15 mini (¾-inch) muffin pan cups with paper baking cups.

2. Prepare cake mix according to package directions. Spoon batter into prepared muffin cups, filling ⅔ full.

3. Bake mini cupcakes 10 to 15 minutes and standard cupcakes 15 to 20 minutes or until cupcakes are golden and toothpick inserted into centers comes out clean. Cool in pans on wire racks 10 minutes. Remove cupcakes to racks; cool completely. Remove paper baking cups.

4. To assemble, frost bottom and side of large cupcakes; coat with coconut. Repeat with mini cupcakes. Attach mini cupcakes to large cupcakes with frosting to form bodies. Attach marshmallows to mini cupcakes with frosting to form heads. Attach inverted peanut butter cups to marshmallows with frosting to form hats. Use pretzels for arms and small cinnamon candies for buttons. Pipe faces with gels. *Makes 15 snowmen*

Holiday

Black Cat Cupcakes

1 package (18¼ ounces) cake mix, any flavor, plus ingredients to prepare mix

1 container (16 ounces) chocolate fudge frosting

Graham crackers

Black string licorice and assorted candies for decoration

1. Preheat oven to 350°F. Line 24 standard (2½-inch) muffin pan cups with paper baking cups.

2. Prepare cake mix according to package directions. Spoon batter into prepared muffin pans, filling ⅔ full.

3. Bake 15 to 20 minutes until toothpick inserted into centers comes out clean. Cool in pans on wire racks 10 minutes. Remove cupcakes to racks; cool completely.

4. Spread tops of cupcakes with frosting. For ears, with serrated knife, carefully cut graham crackers into small triangles as shown in photo; place on cupcakes. Decorate faces with licorice and assorted candies.

Makes 24 cupcakes

Holiday

15

Reindeer Cupcakes

1 package (18¼ ounces) chocolate cake mix, plus ingredients to prepare mix

¼ cup (½ stick) butter, softened

4 cups powdered sugar

5 to 6 tablespoons brewed espresso

½ cup semisweet chocolate chips, melted

1 teaspoon vanilla

Dash salt

24 pretzel twists, broken in half

Assorted candies for decoration

1. Preheat oven to 350°F. Line 24 standard (2½-inch) muffin pan cups with paper baking cups.

2. Prepare cake mix according to package directions. Spoon batter into prepared muffin cups, filling ⅔ full. Bake 15 to 20 minutes or until toothpick inserted into centers comes out clean. Cool in pans on wire racks 10 minutes. Remove cupcakes to racks; cool completely.

3. Beat butter in large bowl with electric mixer at medium speed until creamy. Add powdered sugar and 4 tablespoons espresso; beat until smooth. Add melted chocolate, vanilla and salt; beat until well blended. Add remaining espresso, 1 tablespoon at a time, until frosting is desired consistency.

4. Frost cupcakes. Decorate with broken pretzel pieces for antlers and assorted candies for reindeer faces. *Makes 24 cupcakes*

Holiday

Little Devils

1 package (18¼ ounces) carrot cake mix

½ cup solid-pack pumpkin

⅓ cup vegetable oil

3 eggs

1 container (16 ounces) cream cheese frosting

Assorted Halloween candies, jelly beans, chocolate candies and nuts

1. Preheat oven to 350°F. Line 18 standard (2½-inch) muffin pan cups with paper baking cups.

2. Prepare cake mix according to package directions, using water as directed on package, pumpkin, oil and eggs. Spoon batter into prepared muffin cups, filling ⅔ full. Bake 20 minutes or until toothpick inserted into centers comes out clean. Cool in pans on wire racks 5 minutes. Remove cupcakes to racks; cool completely.

3. Frost cupcakes with cream cheese frosting. Decorate with assorted candies.

Makes 18 cupcakes

Snowy Owl Cupcakes

1 package (18¼ ounces) white cake mix, plus ingredients to prepare mix

1 container (16 ounces) vanilla frosting

2½ cups sweetened shredded coconut

48 round gummy candies

1 tube (0.6 ounce) black piping gel

24 chocolate-covered coffee beans

1. Line 24 standard (2½-inch) muffin pan cups with paper baking cups. Prepare and bake cake mix in prepared muffin cups according to package directions. Cool in pans on wire racks 15 minutes. Remove cupcakes to racks; cool completely.

2. Frost cupcakes with vanilla frosting. Sprinkle coconut over each cupcake, covering completely. Place 2 gummy candies on each cupcake for eyes; dot in center with piping gel. Add chocolate-covered coffee bean for beak.

Makes 24 cupcakes

Scarecrow Cupcakes

1 ¼ cups all-purpose flour

¾ teaspoon baking powder

½ teaspoon baking soda

¾ teaspoon ground cinnamon

⅛ teaspoon *each* ground cloves, nutmeg and allspice

¾ cup heavy cream

2 tablespoons molasses

¼ cup (½ stick) butter, softened

¼ cup *each* granulated sugar and packed brown sugar

2 eggs

½ teaspoon vanilla

¾ cup sweetened shredded coconut

1 container (16 ounces) vanilla frosting

Assorted decors

1. Preheat oven to 350°F. Line 18 standard (2½-inch) muffin pan cups with paper baking cups.

2. Combine flour, baking powder, baking soda and spices in medium bowl. Combine cream and molasses in small bowl. Beat butter in large bowl until creamy. Add sugars; beat until light and fluffy. Add eggs, one at a time, beating after each addition. Blend in vanilla; add flour mixture alternately with cream mixture. Stir in coconut; spoon batter into prepared muffin cups, filling about ½ full.

3. Bake 20 to 25 minutes or until toothpick inserted into centers comes out clean. Cool in pans on wire racks 10 minutes. Remove cupcakes to racks; cool completely. Frost and decorate as desired.   *Makes 18 cupcakes*

Holiday

Leprechaun Cupcakes

1 package (18¼ ounces) yellow or white cake mix plus ingredients to prepare mix

1 container (16 ounces) vanilla frosting

   Green, orange and red gumdrops

   Black decorating gel

   Mini candy-coated chocolate pieces

1. Preheat oven to 350°F. Line 24 standard (2½-inch) muffin pan cups with paper baking cups. Prepare cake mix according to package directions. Spoon batter into prepared muffin cups, filling ⅔ full.

2. Bake 15 to 20 minutes or until toothpick inserted into centers comes out clean. Cool in pans on wire racks 10 minutes. Remove cupcakes to racks; cool completely.

3. Roll out green gumdrops on generously sugared surface. Cut out pieces to resemble hats. Pipe gel onto hats for hatbands; place candies on hatbands for buckles. Place hats on cupcakes. Roll out orange gumdrops on generously sugared surface. Cut out pieces to resemble sideburns and beards; place on cupcakes. Roll out red gumdrops on generously sugared surface. Cut out small pieces to resemble mouths; place on cupcakes. Place candies on cupcakes for eyes.

Makes 24 cupcakes

Spider Cupcakes

1 package (18¼ ounces) yellow or white cake mix

1 cup solid-pack pumpkin

¾ cup water

3 eggs

2 tablespoons vegetable oil

1 teaspoon *each* ground cinnamon and pumpkin pie spice

Orange food coloring

1 container (16 ounces) vanilla, cream cheese or caramel frosting

4 ounces semisweet chocolate

48 black gumdrops

1. Preheat oven to 350°F. Line 24 standard (2½-inch) muffin pan cups with paper baking cups.

2. Beat cake mix, pumpkin, water, eggs, oil and spices in large bowl with electric mixer at medium speed 3 minutes. Spoon batter into prepared muffin cups, filling ¼ full.

3. Bake 20 minutes or until toothpick inserted into centers comes out clean. Cool in pans on wire racks 10 minutes. Remove cupcakes to racks; cool completely.

4. Add food coloring to frosting, a few drops at a time, until desired color is reached. Frost cupcakes. Place chocolate in small resealable food storage bag. Microwave on MEDIUM (50% power) 40 seconds. Knead bag; heat 30 seconds more or until melted. Cut off tiny corner of bag; drizzle chocolate in four concentric circles over top of cupcakes. Immediately draw 8 lines at regular intervals from center to edges of cupcakes with knife to create web. Place one gumdrop in center of web. Roll out another gumdrop on sugared surface. Slice thinly; roll into legs. Arrange around gumdrop to make spider.

Makes 24 cupcakes

Cookies & Cream Cupcakes

2¼ cups all-purpose flour

1 tablespoon baking powder

½ teaspoon salt

1⅔ cups sugar

1 cup milk

½ cup (1 stick) butter, softened

2 teaspoons vanilla

3 egg whites

1 cup crushed chocolate sandwich cookies (about 10 cookies) plus additional for garnish

1 container (16 ounces) vanilla frosting

1. Preheat oven to 350°F. Lightly grease 24 standard (2½-inch) muffin pan cups or line with paper baking cups.

2. Sift flour, baking powder and salt together in large bowl. Stir in sugar. Add milk, butter and vanilla; beat with electric mixer at low speed 30 seconds. Beat at medium speed 2 minutes. Add egg whites; beat 2 minutes. Stir in 1 cup crushed cookies. Spoon batter evenly into prepared muffin cups, filling ⅔ full.

3. Bake 20 to 25 minutes or until toothpick inserted into centers comes out clean. Cool in pans on wire racks 10 minutes. Remove cupcakes to racks; cool completely.

4. Frost cupcakes; top with additional crushed cookies.

Makes 24 cupcakes

Lazy Daisy Cupcakes

1 package (18¼ ounces) yellow cake mix, plus ingredients to prepare mix

Yellow food coloring

1 container (16 ounces) vanilla frosting

30 large marshmallows

24 jelly beans

1. Line 24 standard (2½-inch) muffin pan cups with paper baking cups. Prepare and bake cake mix in prepared muffin cups according to package directions. Cool in pans on wire racks 15 minutes. Remove cupcakes to racks; cool completely.

2. Add food coloring to frosting, a few drops at a time, until desired color is reached. Frost cooled cupcakes with tinted frosting.

3. Cut each marshmallow crosswise into 4 pieces with scissors. Stretch pieces into petal shapes; place 5 pieces on each cupcake to form flower. Place candy in center of each flower.   *Makes 24 cupcakes*

Peanut Butter & Jam Muffins

2 cups all-purpose flour

2 teaspoons baking powder

1 teaspoon baking soda

2 eggs

½ cup creamy peanut butter

¾ cup thawed frozen unsweetened apple juice concentrate

¼ cup milk

¼ cup (½ stick) butter, melted

½ cup chopped salted peanuts

6 tablespoons strawberry jam

1. Preheat oven to 350°F. Grease 12 standard (2½-inch) muffin pan cups.

2. Combine dry ingredients in medium bowl. Beat together eggs and peanut butter in separate medium bowl until smooth. Blend in apple juice concentrate, milk and butter. Add to dry ingredients; mix just until moistened. Stir in peanuts. Spoon half of batter evenly into prepared muffin cups. Drop 1½ teaspoons strawberry fruit spread into center of each cup; cover with remaining batter.

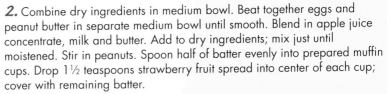

3. Bake 18 minutes or until golden brown. Cool in pan on wire rack 5 minutes. Remove muffins to rack; cool completely.

Makes 12 muffins

Butterfly Cupcakes

1 package (18¼ ounces) cake mix, any flavor, plus ingredients to prepare mix

1 container (16 ounces) white frosting

Blue and green food coloring

Mini candy-coated chocolate pieces and colored sugar

Red licorice ropes, cut into 4-inch pieces

1. Preheat oven to 350°F. Lightly spray 24 standard (2½-inch) muffin pan cups with nonstick cooking spray.

2. Prepare cake mix according to package directions. Spoon batter into prepared muffin cups, filling ⅔ full. Bake about 20 minutes or until toothpick inserted into centers comes out clean. Cool in pans on wire racks 10 minutes. Remove cupcakes to racks; cool completely.

3. Divide frosting equally between 2 small bowls. Add food coloring to each bowl, one drop at a time, until desired color is reached.

4. Cut cupcakes in half. Place cupcake halves together, cut sides out, to resemble butterfly wings. Frost with desired colors; decorate with chocolate pieces and colored sugar as desired. Snip each end of licorice rope pieces to form antennae; place in center of each cupcake.

Makes 24 cupcakes

Play Ball

2 cups plus 1 tablespoon all-purpose flour, divided
¾ cup *each* **granulated sugar and packed brown sugar**
1 tablespoon baking powder
1 teaspoon salt
½ teaspoon baking soda
1¼ cups milk
½ cup shortening
3 eggs
1½ teaspoons vanilla
½ cup mini semisweet chocolate chips
1 container (16 ounces) vanilla frosting
Assorted candies and food colorings

1. Preheat oven to 350°F. Line 24 standard (2½-inch) muffin pan cups with paper baking cups.

2. Combine 2 cups flour, sugars, baking powder, salt and baking soda in medium bowl. Beat milk, shortening, eggs and vanilla in large bowl with electric mixer at medium speed until well blended. Add flour mixture; blend well. Beat at high speed 3 minutes. Toss mini chocolate chips with remaining 1 tablespoon flour; stir into batter. Divide evenly among prepared muffin cups.

3. Bake 20 minutes or until toothpick inserted into centers comes out clean. Cool in pans on wire racks 5 minutes. Remove cupcakes to racks; cool completely. Decorate with desired frostings and candies to resemble baseballs, basketballs or soccer balls. *Makes 24 cupcakes*

Peanut Butter Surprise

2 cups all-purpose flour

2 teaspoons baking powder

¼ teaspoon salt

1¾ cups sugar

½ cup (1 stick) butter, softened

¾ cup whole milk

1 teaspoon vanilla

3 egg whites

2 bars (3 ounces each) bittersweet chocolate candy, melted

30 mini peanut butter cups

1 container (16 ounces) chocolate frosting

3 squares (1 ounce each) white chocolate, chopped

1. Preheat oven to 350°F. Grease 30 standard (2½-inch) muffin pan cups.

2. Combine flour, baking powder and salt in medium bowl; mix well. Beat sugar and butter in large bowl with electric mixer at medium speed 1 minute. Add milk and vanilla; gradually beat in flour mixture until well blended. Add egg whites; beat 1 minute. Stir in cooled candy. Spoon 1 heaping tablespoon batter into each muffin cup. Place one peanut butter cup in center of each cupcake. Spoon 1 heaping tablespoon batter over peanut butter cup.

3. Bake 24 to 26 minutes. Cool in pans on wire racks 10 minutes. Remove cupcakes to racks; cool completely.

4. Spread frosting over cupcakes. Place white chocolate in small resealable food storage bag. Microwave on HIGH 40 seconds. Turn bag over; microwave additional 30 seconds. Cut off tiny corner of bag; drizzle white chocolate over frosted cupcakes.

Makes 30 cupcakes

Cinnamon Spiced Muffins

1½ cups all-purpose flour

¾ cup sugar, divided

2 teaspoons baking powder

½ teaspoon *each* salt, ground nutmeg, ground coriander and ground allspice

½ cup milk

⅓ cup plus ¼ cup (½ stick) butter, melted, divided

1 egg

1 teaspoon ground cinnamon

1. Preheat oven to 400°F. Grease 36 mini (1¾-inch) muffin cups.

2. Combine flour, ½ cup sugar, baking powder, salt and spices in large bowl. Combine milk, ⅓ cup butter and egg in small bowl; stir into flour mixture just until moistened. Spoon evenly into prepared muffin cups.

3. Bake 10 to 13 minutes or until edges are lightly browned and toothpick inserted into centers comes out clean. Remove from pan to wire rack.

4. Meanwhile, combine remaining ¼ cup sugar and cinnamon in shallow dish. Dip warm muffin tops in ¼ cup melted butter, then in sugar-cinnamon mixture. Serve warm. *Makes 3 dozen muffins*

Cubcakes

- 1 package (18¼ ounces) chocolate cake mix, plus ingredients to prepare mix
- 1 container (16 ounces) chocolate frosting
- 1 package (5 ounces) chocolate nonpareil candies
- 72 red cinnamon candies
  - Chocolate sprinkles
  - Black decorating gel

1. Line 24 standard (2½-inch) muffin pan cups with paper baking cups.

2. Prepare and bake cake mix according to package directions. Cool in pans on wire racks 15 minutes. Remove cupcakes to racks; cool completely.

3. Frost cooled cupcakes with chocolate frosting. Use nonpareils to make ears and muzzle. Add red candies for eyes and nose. Sprinkle with chocolate sprinkles for fur. Use decorating gel to place dots on eyes and create mouth.

Makes 24 cupcakes

Birthday

29

Ice Cream Cone Cakes

1 package (18¼ ounces) devil's food cake mix, plus ingredients to prepare mix

⅓ cup sour cream

18 flat-bottomed ice cream cones, assorted colors

1¼ cups frozen yogurt (any flavor)

Assorted sprinkles

1. Preheat oven to 350°F. Grease and flour 8- or 9-inch round cake pan.

2. Prepare cake mix according to package directions, substituting sour cream for ⅓ cup water and decreasing oil to ¼ cup. Spoon ½ of batter (about 2⅓ cups) evenly into ice cream cones, using about 2 tablespoons batter for each. Pour remaining batter into prepared cake pan.

3. Stand cones on cookie sheet. Bake cones and cake layer until toothpick inserted into center of cake comes out clean, about 20 minutes for cones and about 35 minutes for cake layer. Cool on wire racks, removing cake from pan after 10 minutes. Reserve or freeze cake layer for another use.

4. Top each filled cone with ¼ cup scoop of frozen yogurt just before serving. Top with sprinkles. Serve immediately. *Makes 18 cone cakes*

Peppermint Cupcakes

1 package (18¼ ounces) white cake mix

1⅓ cups water

3 egg whites

2 tablespoons vegetable oil or melted butter

½ teaspoon peppermint extract

3 to 4 drops red liquid food coloring *or* ¼ teaspoon gel food coloring

1 container (16 ounces) prepared vanilla frosting

½ cup crushed peppermint candies (about 16 candies)

1. Preheat oven to 350°F. Line 30 standard (2½-inch) muffin pan cups with paper baking cups.

2. Beat cake mix, water, egg whites, oil, peppermint extract and food coloring in large bowl with electric mixer at low speed 30 seconds. Beat at medium speed 2 minutes. Spoon batter into prepared muffin cups, filling ¾ full.

3. Bake 20 to 22 minutes or until toothpick inserted into centers comes out clean. Cool in pans on wire racks 10 minutes. Remove cupcakes to racks; cool completely.

4. Spread frosting over cooled cupcakes; sprinkle with crushed candies. Store at room temperature up to 24 hours or cover and refrigerate up to 3 days before serving.

Makes 30 cupcakes

Surprise Package Cupcakes

1 package (18¼ ounces) chocolate cake mix, plus ingredients to prepare mix

1 container (16 ounces) vanilla frosting

Food coloring (optional)

1 tube (4¼ ounces) white decorating icing

72 chewy fruit squares

Colored sprinkles and birthday candles (optional)

1. Spray 24 standard (2½-inch) muffin pan cups with nonstick cooking spray. Prepare and bake cake mix in prepared muffin cups according to package directions. Cool in pans on wire racks 15 minutes. Remove cupcakes to racks; cool completely.

2. Tint frosting with food coloring, if desired, adding a few drops at a time until desired color is reached. Spread frosting over cupcakes.

3. Use decorating icing to pipe ribbons on fruit squares to resemble wrapped presents. Place 3 candy presents on each cupcake. Decorate with sprinkles and candles.

Makes 24 cupcakes

Toffee Crunch Muffins

1½ cups all-purpose flour

⅓ cup packed brown sugar

2 teaspoons baking powder

½ teaspoon *each* baking soda and salt

½ cup *each* milk and sour cream

1 egg, beaten

3 tablespoons butter, melted

1 teaspoon vanilla

3 bars (1.4 ounces each) chocolate-covered toffee, chopped, divided

1. Preheat oven to 400°F. Grease 36 mini (1¾-inch) muffin cups.

2. Combine flour, sugar, baking powder, baking soda and salt in large bowl. Combine milk, sour cream, egg, butter and vanilla in small bowl until well blended. Stir into flour mixture just until moistened. Fold in ⅔ of toffee. Spoon batter into prepared muffin cups, filling almost full. Sprinkle evenly with remaining toffee.

3. Bake 16 to 18 minutes or until toothpick inserted into centers comes out clean. Remove from pans; cool on wire racks 10 minutes.

Makes 36 mini muffins

Birthday

Carrot Cream Cheese Cupcakes

1 package (8 ounces) cream cheese, softened

¼ cup powdered sugar

1 package (18¼ ounces) spice cake mix, plus ingredients to prepare mix

2 cups grated carrots

2 tablespoons finely chopped candied ginger

1 container (16 ounces) cream cheese frosting

3 tablespoons maple syrup

Orange peel strips (optional)

1. Preheat oven to 350°F. Spray 14 jumbo (3½-inch) muffin pan cups with nonstick cooking spray.

2. Beat cream cheese and powdered sugar in large bowl with electric mixer at medium speed 1 minute or until light and fluffy. Cover and refrigerate.

3. Prepare cake mix according to package directions; stir in carrots and ginger. Spoon batter into prepared muffin cups, filling ⅓ full (about ¼ cup batter). Place 1 tablespoon cream cheese mixture in center of each cup. Top with remaining batter up to ⅔ full.

4. Bake 25 to 28 minutes or until toothpick inserted into centers comes out clean. Cool in pans on wire racks 10 minutes. Remove cupcakes to racks; cool completely.

5. Mix frosting and maple syrup until well blended. Frost tops of cupcakes; top with orange peel.

Makes 14 cupcakes

Magical Wizard Hats

1 package (18¼ ounces) cake mix, any flavor, plus ingredients to prepare mix

2 containers (16 ounces each) vanilla frosting

Yellow and black food colorings

2 packages (4 ounces each) sugar cones

Orange sugar, decors and black decorating gel

1. Preheat oven to 350°F. Line 24 standard (2½-inch) muffin pan cups with paper baking cups.

2. Prepare and bake cake mix in prepared muffin cups according to package directions. Cool in pans on wire racks 15 minutes. Remove cupcakes to racks; cool completely.

3. Frost cupcakes. Place ½ cup remaining frosting in small bowl; tint with yellow food coloring. Tint remaining frosting with black food coloring. Spread sugar cones with dark frosting, covering completely. Place 1 cone upside down on each frosted cupcake. Spoon yellow frosting into small resealable food storage bag. Cut off small corner of bag; pipe yellow frosting around base of each frosted cone. Decorate with orange sugar, decors and decorating gel.

Makes 24 cupcakes

Birthday 35

Marmalade Muffins

2 cups all-purpose flour

2 teaspoons baking powder

¾ teaspoon salt

1 cup (2 sticks) unsalted butter, softened

1½ cups sugar

2 eggs

1½ teaspoons vanilla

1 cup orange marmalade, plus additional for topping

1 cup buttermilk

1. Preheat oven to 350°F. Line 18 standard (2½-inch) muffin pan cups with paper baking cups.

2. Sift flour, baking powder and salt in medium bowl; set aside. Beat butter and sugar in large bowl with electric mixer on high speed about 5 minutes until light and fluffy. Add eggs one at a time and beat until blended. Add vanilla; mix well. Fold in half of dry mixture. Stir in buttermilk; do not overmix. marmalade and remaining dry mixture.

3. Spoon batter into prepared muffin cups, filling ¾ full. Bake 20 to 25 minutes or until edges are golden brown and toothpick inserted into centers comes out clean. Top with additional marmalade.

Makes 18 muffins

Strawberry Muffins

1 ¼ cups all-purpose flour
2 ½ teaspoons baking powder
½ teaspoon salt
1 cup uncooked old-fashioned oats
½ cup sugar
1 cup milk
½ cup (1 stick) butter, melted
1 egg, beaten
1 teaspoon vanilla
1 cup chopped fresh strawberries

1. Preheat oven to 425°F. Line 12 standard (2½-inch) muffin pan cups with paper baking cups.

2. Combine flour, baking powder and salt in large bowl. Stir in oats and sugar. Combine milk, butter, egg and vanilla in small bowl until well blended; stir into flour mixture just until moistened. Fold in strawberries. Spoon into prepared muffin cups, filling about ⅔ full.

3. Bake 15 to 18 minutes or until lightly browned and toothpick inserted into centers comes out clean. Remove muffins from pan to wire racks; Cool 10 minutes.

Makes 12 muffins

Fruit

Apple Streusel
Mini Muffins

¼ **cup chopped pecans**
2 **tablespoons brown sugar**
1 **tablespoon all-purpose flour**
2 **teaspoons butter, melted**
1 **package (7 ounces) apple-cinnamon muffin mix**
½ **cup shredded peeled apple**

1. Preheat oven to 425°F. Coat 18 mini (1¾-inch) muffin cups with nonstick cooking spray.

2. Combine pecans, brown sugar, flour and butter in small bowl.

3. Prepare muffin mix according to package directions. Stir in apple. Fill each muffin cup ⅔ full. Sprinkle approximately 1 teaspoon pecan mixture on top of each muffin. Bake 12 to 15 minutes or until golden brown. Cool slightly. Serve warm.   *Makes 18 mini muffins*

Blueberry White Chip Muffins

2 cups all-purpose flour

½ cup granulated sugar

¼ cup packed brown sugar

2½ teaspoons baking powder

½ teaspoon salt

¾ cup milk

1 large egg, lightly beaten

¼ cup (½ stick) butter or margarine, melted

½ teaspoon grated lemon peel

2 cups (12-ounce package) NESTLÉ® TOLL HOUSE® Premier White Morsels, *divided*

1½ cups fresh or frozen blueberries

Streusel Topping (recipe follows)

PREHEAT oven to 375°F. Paper-line 18 muffin cups.

COMBINE flour, granulated sugar, brown sugar, baking powder and salt in large bowl. Stir in milk, egg, butter and lemon peel. Stir in *1½ cups* morsels and blueberries. Spoon into prepared muffin cups, filling almost full. Sprinkle with Streusel Topping.

BAKE for 22 to 25 minutes or until wooden pick inserted in center comes out clean. Cool in pans for 5 minutes; remove to wire racks to cool slightly.

PLACE *remaining* morsels in small, *heavy-duty* resealable plastic food storage bag. Microwave on MEDIUM-HIGH (70%) power for 30 seconds; knead. Microwave at additional 10- to 15-second intervals, kneading until smooth. Cut tiny corner from bag; squeeze to drizzle over muffins. Serve warm.

Makes 18 muffins

Streusel Topping: COMBINE ⅓ cup granulated sugar, ¼ cup all-purpose flour and ¼ teaspoon ground cinnamon in small bowl. Cut in 3 tablespoons butter or margarine with pastry blender or two knives until mixture resembles coarse crumbs.

Fruit

Banana Split Cupcakes

1 package (18¼ ounces) yellow cake mix, divided
1 cup *each* mashed ripe bananas and water
3 eggs
1 cup chopped drained maraschino cherries
1½ cups mini semisweet chocolate chips, divided
1½ cups prepared vanilla frosting
1 cup marshmallow creme
1 teaspoon shortening
30 whole maraschino cherries, drained and patted dry

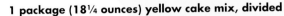

1. Preheat oven to 350°F. Line 30 standard (2½-inch) muffin pan cups with paper baking cups.

2. Reserve 2 tablespoons cake mix. Combine remaining cake mix, water, bananas and eggs in large bowl. Beat at low speed of electric mixer about 30 seconds or until moistened. Beat at medium speed 2 minutes. Combine chopped cherries and reserved cake mix in small bowl. Stir chopped cherry mixture and 1 cup chocolate chips into batter. Spoon batter into prepared muffin cups, filling ⅔ full.

3. Bake 15 to 20 minutes or until toothpick inserted into centers comes out clean. Cool in pans on wire racks 10 minutes. Remove cupcakes to racks; cool completely.

4. Combine frosting and marshmallow creme in medium bowl until blended. Frost cupcakes. Combine remaining ½ cup chocolate chips and shortening in small microwavable bowl. Microwave on HIGH 30 to 45 seconds, stirring after 30 seconds. Drizzle chocolate mixture over cupcakes. Place one whole cherry on each cupcake.   *Makes 30 cupcakes*

Caramel Apple Cupcakes

1 package (18¼ ounces) yellow or butter cake mix, plus ingredients to prepare mix

1 cup chopped dried apples

Caramel Frosting (recipe follows)

Chopped pecans

1. Preheat oven to 375°F. Line 24 standard (2½-inch) muffin pan cups with paper baking cups.

2. Prepare cake mix according to package directions. Stir in apples. Spoon batter into prepared muffin cups, filling ⅔ full. Bake 15 to 20 minutes or until toothpick inserted into centers comes out clean. Cool in pans on wire racks 10 minutes. Remove cupcakes to racks; cool completely.

3. Prepare Caramel Frosting. Frost cupcakes; sprinkle with pecans.

Makes 24 cupcakes

Caramel Frosting: Melt 3 tablespoons butter in 2-quart saucepan. Stir in 1 cup packed light brown sugar, ½ cup evaporated milk and ⅛ teaspoon salt. Bring to a boil, stirring constantly. Remove from heat; cool to lukewarm. Add 3¾ cups powdered sugar; beat until frosting is of spreading consistency. Add ¾ teaspoon vanilla; beat until smooth. Makes about 5 cups.

Fruit

Cheese & Apple Muffins

2 cups buttermilk baking mix
½ to 1 teaspoon ground red pepper
½ teaspoon salt
⅔ cup milk
1 egg, lightly beaten
1 medium apple, peeled, cored and grated
1 cup (4 ounces) shredded sharp Cheddar cheese

1. Preheat oven to 375°F. Spray 12 standard (2½-inch) muffin pan cups with nonstick cooking spray.

2. Combine baking mix, red pepper and salt in large bowl. Add milk and egg; mix until just moistened. *Do not overmix.* Fold in apple and cheese. Spoon batter into prepared muffin cups, filling ¾ full.

3. Bake 20 to 25 minutes or until golden brown. Cool 5 minutes in pan. Remove muffins from pan to wire rack. Serve warm.

Makes 12 muffins

Fruit

Morning Muffins with Blueberries

½ cup plus 1 tablespoon sugar, divided
⅛ teaspoon ground cinnamon
1¾ cups all-purpose flour
 2 teaspoons baking powder
½ teaspoon salt
½ cup milk
¼ cup vegetable oil
 1 egg
1 teaspoon vanilla
1 teaspoon grated orange peel
1 cup fresh or frozen blueberries, thawed and dried

1. Preheat oven to 400°F. Grease 12 standard (2½-inch) muffin pan cups. Combine 1 tablespoon sugar and cinnamon in small bowl; set aside.

2. Combine flour, remaining ½ cup sugar, baking powder and salt in large bowl. Beat milk, oil, egg, vanilla and orange peel in small bowl until blended. Make well in center of flour mixture; stir in milk mixture just until moistened. Fold in blueberries. Spoon evenly into prepared muffin cups, filling about ⅔ full.

3. Bake 15 to 18 minutes or until toothpick inserted into centers comes out clean. Immediately sprinkle sugar mixture over hot muffins. Transfer to wire racks. Serve warm. *Makes 12 muffins*

Fruit

Vanilla-Strawberry Cupcakes

2 cups all-purpose flour
2 teaspoons baking powder
¼ teaspoon salt
1¾ cups granulated sugar
¾ cup (1½ sticks) butter, softened and divided
¾ cup milk
3½ teaspoons vanilla, divided
3 egg whites
½ cup strawberry preserves
1 package (8 ounces) cream cheese, chilled and cut into cubes
2 cups powdered sugar
1 to 1½ cups sliced fresh strawberries

1. Preheat oven to 350°F. Lightly grease 28 standard (2½-inch) muffin pan cups.

2. Combine flour, baking powder and salt in medium bowl; mix well. Beat granulated sugar and ½ cup butter in large bowl with electric mixer at medium speed 1 minute. Add milk and 1½ teaspoons vanilla. Beat at low speed 30 seconds. Gradually beat in flour mixture; beat at medium speed 2 minutes. Add egg whites; beat 1 minute. Spoon batter into prepared muffin cups, filling ½ full. Drop 1 teaspoon preserves on top of batter; swirl into batter with toothpick.

3. Bake 20 to 22 minutes or until toothpick inserted into centers comes out clean. Cool in pans on wire racks 10 minutes. Remove cupcakes to racks; cool completely.

4. Process cream cheese, remaining ¼ cup butter and remaining 2 teaspoons vanilla in food processor just until blended. Add powdered sugar; pulse just until sugar is incorporated. (Do not overmix or frosting will be too soft to spread). Spread frosting over cooled cupcakes; decorate with sliced strawberries. *Makes 28 cupcakes*

Chocolate Cherry Cups

⅓ **cup all-purpose flour**

⅓ **cup sugar**

¼ **cup ground baking chocolate**

¼ **cup cocoa powder**

¼ **teaspoon baking powder**

¼ **teaspoon salt**

6 **ounces nonfat vanilla yogurt**

3 **egg whites**

½ **teaspoon almond extract**

36 **thawed, drained pitted sour cherries, frozen without sugar**

1. Preheat oven to 350°F. Line 12 standard (2½-inch) muffin pan cups with foil baking cups.

2. Place flour, sugar, ground chocolate, cocoa powder, baking powder and salt in medium bowl. Whisk until combined. Beat egg whites in medium bowl with electric mixer at high speed until soft peaks form. Add yogurt to dry mixture. Stir well, scraping sides of bowl. Fold in beaten egg whites and almond extract. Spoon batter into prepared muffin cups, filling ⅔ full. Place 3 cherries into each cup, pressing lightly into batter.

3. Bake 20 to 25 minutes, until tops are puffy and edges are set. Centers will be moist.   *Makes 12 cupcakes*

Fruit

Lemon Poppy Seed Muffins

3 cups all-purpose flour

1 cup sugar

3 tablespoons poppy seeds

1 tablespoon grated lemon peel

2 teaspoons baking powder

1 teaspoon baking soda

½ teaspoon salt

1 container (16 ounces) plain low-fat yogurt

½ cup fresh lemon juice

2 eggs, beaten

¼ cup vegetable oil

1½ teaspoons vanilla

1. Preheat oven to 400°F. Lightly grease 12 jumbo (3½-inch) muffin pan cups.

2. Combine flour, sugar, poppy seeds, lemon peel, baking powder, baking soda and salt in large bowl; stir until blended. Combine yogurt, lemon juice, eggs, oil and vanilla in small bowl; stir until well blended. Stir yogurt mixture into flour mixture just until moistened. Spoon batter into prepared muffin cups, filling ⅔ full.

3. Bake 25 to 30 minutes or until toothpick inserted into centers comes out clean. Cool in pans on wire racks 5 minutes. Remove from pans. Cool on wire racks 10 minutes.   *Makes 12 jumbo muffins*

Fruit